THURSDAY'S CHILD

My Journey So Far

A memoir

Peagie Foday

Sierra Leonean Writers Series

Thursday's Child: My Journey So Far

ISBN: 978-9988-8779-0-3

Sierra Leonean Writers Series
Warima / Freetown / Accra
120 Kissy Road, Freetown, Sierra Leone
Kofi Annan Avenue, North Legon, Accra
Publisher: Prof. Osman Sankoh (Mallam O.)
publisher@sl-writers-series.org
www.sl-writers-series.org

ACKNOWLEDGEMENTS

I would like to thank my friends and family who, for the sake of authenticity, have allowed me to name them in my story, and all who have helped me realize my dream of setting up the Peagie Woobay Scholarship Fund…for the love of the girls.

I am also deeply grateful to the following family members who, despite the pain I caused them as a teenager, gave me loving support throughout that trying period: my parents, David and Agnes Woobay, my older sisters, Sentho and Yemah Woobay, and my aunt, Lucy Berewa. Florella Hazeley has to be included in this list. In my distress, she comforted me with the promise that all was not lost. David

Muhlemann, you came into my life much too early, but I have never regretted having my wonderful son.

I am also grateful for the love and unending support I receive from my husband, Emmanuel Foday, and from my daughter, Manelle, who is always willing to dance at fund-raising events for the Peagie Woobay Scholarship Fund.

Finally, this memoir might never have seen the light of day, but for the encouragement I received from 'aunty' Lucilda Hunter who also helped me through the process. Thank you so much.

DEDICATION

To the late Dr. Theresa Ganda who took care of me with such kindness and competence during my pregnancy at the early age of fifteen.

FOREWORD

The writer and "child" in question is a dear friend of mine whom I initially met at the Annie Walsh Memorial School in Freetown, Sierra Leone and later at Fourah Bay College, University of Sierra Leone. I am totally in awe of this protagonist, whose passion for the development of girls has surpassed her own very expectations. Her unrivalled enthusiasm, commitment and zeal to break the cycle of discrimination, social de-clusion, frustration, depression, bullying and undue pressure on vulnerable girls are clearly illustrated in this memoir.

We are given a visceral portrayal of her arduous and agonizing journey precipitated by her getting pregnant at the tender age of fifteen. The reader is offered no choice but to feel the anguish caused by the stigma brought on by ingrained social and cultural expectations of a girl child, an unmarried female, a Sherbro…, that this character has undergone. One is also liberated by the affirmation that the support of parents, family members and true friends eventually see people through the most difficult of situations.

Peagie has been exceptional in her fervor and drive for empowering young girls, especially girls who need a second chance. Second chances do not easily come to everyone and the need for girls especially to understand that having an education is the key to success, to a better life, to a stable and secure future for themselves and their children and to a better, sustainable and healthy life for themselves and their families.

As a ***Thursday's child***, who has far to go, the journey is just started for this writer. There will be more to come and more to write about and anyone who reads this book will want to be part of the other story. "For the love of the girls", being her best phrase, the continued support for the schooling, the care and the welfare of the girls and their children is the base of the next volume of **Thursday's Child.** I have been inspired by this book and definitely look forward to reading more from this expressive author. I hope every girl and in fact everyone reading this will even be more inspired.

Dr. Fatou Taqi

President

50/50 Group (SL)

Chapter One

A Privileged childhood

I was born in Kenema in the Eastern Province of Sierra Leone, on the 7th of May, 1971. That was ten years after independence, and Sierra Leone was a stable and prosperous country, or so it seemed to me. I was the last of three children—all girls. My older sisters, Sentho and Yemah were five and four years older than me respectively. My dad, David Woobay, was a civil servant. We called him 'the king' because though he was an only child, it seemed that he took care of everybody in his home town which was Temdel in Moyamba District. He and I share the same birthday, which might account for the special bond there has always been between us. Though he showed equal love to us all, he and I clicked in a special way; so much so that I wanted to look just like him, and cried if my hair was not cut as low as his. My mum, Agnes Woobay, née Berewa, was a schoolteacher, and originally from Bumpe in Bo District. Our household included older relations who called her 'Aunty', so my sisters and I did the same. When I was two years old, my dad was transferred to Bo Town, where my mother's sister, Lucy, was living at the time. She was a nurse in government service and could therefore be transferred to other towns as considered necessary. Oddly enough, her own children called her 'Mummy', so once again, my sisters and I followed suit; our mother was 'Aunty', and our aunt, 'Mummy'.

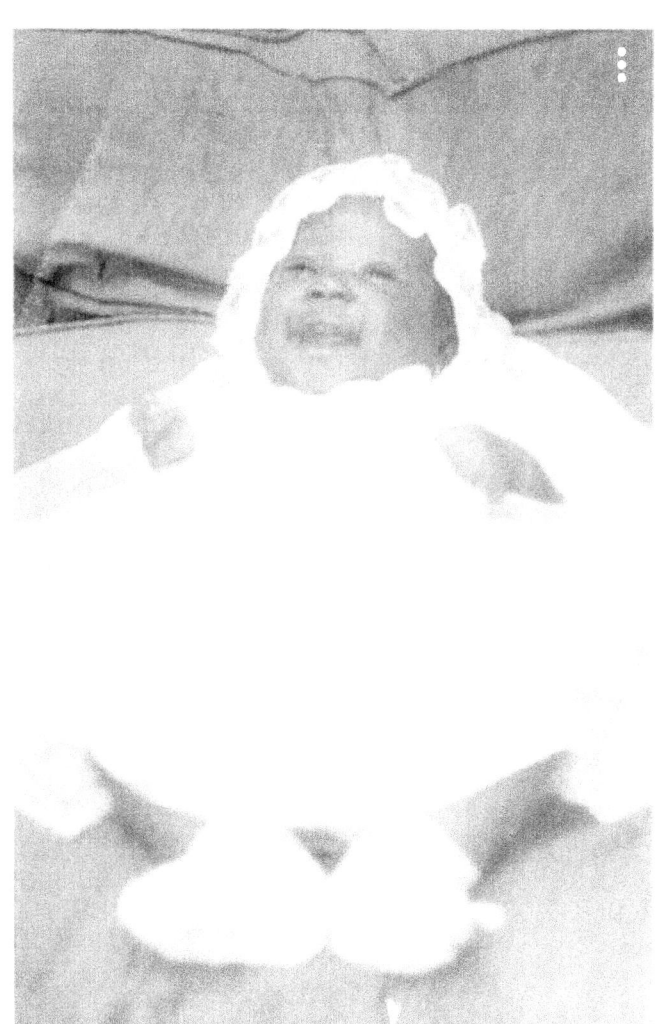

Peagie at 6 months

3

We lived in government quarters in an exclusive area called The Reservation. In those days, things worked well in Sierra Leone, so we enjoyed such modern amenities as twenty-four-hour electricity and pipe-borne water indoors. Our clean bathroom, also indoors, had a shower, and how we children enjoyed it! Twice a day. My cousin Mahen and I went for refreshing showers and took so long that our late Grandma Dina would have to shout at us to vacate the bathroom.

Our daily schedule was as it was for all school-going children in Sierra Leone when school hours were from 8 a.m to 2 p.m. After school, we had a meal, rested, played, and studied—generally in that order—from 4 p.m. to 6 p.m. Then, we watched television from 7 p.m. to 8.30 p.m. Yes, though all the programmes were in black and white, Sierra Leone had a functioning television system that covered a lot of the country. Some years later, an

4

uncle of ours, Joe Genda Bassie, was kind enough to gift the family with our first colour TV. Growing up in Bo was an experience also memorable for the fun we had attending garden parties at the Bo Club House, watching movies at the Rio or Rex cinemas, and taking holiday trips to visit to our uncles Solomon and Alfred Berewa in Freetown (the capital city) and Kenema, respectively. We usually travelled by bus, but a domestic airline existed in those days so we sometimes made the trips by air, courtesy of another of our uncles, the late R.B. Fallah. We always looked forward to those holiday visits because, unlike our mother who was quite a disciplinarian, our wonderful 'Mummy' (Aunty Lucy) spoiled us quite a bit with gifts whenever we visited a town to which she had been transferred. Those gifts always included new dresses in our favourite colours; at the time, mine was orange.

Peagie at 5yrs, 3rd right, 2nd row

My parents owned a Volkswagen Beetle with the registration number SM 644, and my mum was one of the first female drivers in Bo. The Woobay girls went to school by car in a country where less than 2% of the population owned private vehicles and most children walked to and from school, some for miles. My sisters and I thought we were rich but later discovered that far from being rich, our parents simply tried to give us the best life they could afford.

I attended the Roman Catholic Model School where I excelled because, though I was always much naughtier than my older sisters, right from the start I loved books and learning. When my teachers told my parents how intelligent I was and that they expected me to go far educationally, my proud mum said, as if that explained everything,

"Peagie was born on a Thursday. Thursday's child has far to go."

(She was referring to a line from an old English nursery rhyme that begins, Monday's Child is fair of face…). As for 'the king', he praised me so often that people began to say openly that I was his favourite child. Life in Bo was so pleasant, that we were not happy when our father was transferred to Freetown, especially since our mum and Sentho had to stay behind, 'Aunty' on account of her job, and Sentho, because she was now a senior student at the UCC Secondary School.

Chapter Two

We move to Freetown

It took us a while to settle down in Freetown because even though his transfer had been confirmed long before his departure from Bo, my dad had not been assigned government quarters. The family had to split up further. I went with him to live with his cousin, Uncle Joe (Genda Bassie) at the Public Works Department (PWD) compound behind the Pademba Road Prison, while my sister, Yemah, also in secondary school, went to live with our great uncle, Solomon Berewa, in King Tom which was another part of town. By this time, the standard of living had started to drop in the country, partly because we hosted the annual conference of the

9

Organization of African Unity (O.A.U) in 1980. Doing so had involved huge government expenditure to give Freetown a facelift, and to provide board and lodging for all the delegates as well as the international press. Generally, African countries that hosted the O.A.U. conference had either gone into debt or greatly depleted their national reserves. Sierra Leone was no exception. After the conference, the country started experiencing an economic decline, with inflation and deterioration of its infrastructure. But in spite of this, on a personal level life was still good, though we greatly missed being together as a family. I thank my late Aunty Hannah for the good care she took of me, Uncle Joe for always smiling, and my cousin, Larry Bassie who, though always fun to be with, advised me to study hard, saying that hard work was the way to succeed in life. Larry used to study till the wee hours of the morning and was a real brain box.

The PWD compound was a lovely place, in a pleasant neighbourhood. And we had great neighbours, some of whom I still remember, for example, the Jalloh-Jamboria, Muhlemann, Brown, Jawarah, Iscandri, and French families. All of them had school-going children of about my age. We went to school together and afterwards, had fun.

Eventually, my father found a place of his own at Smart Farm, off Wilkinson Road, and, since Sentho had now finished secondary school, once again all the family, except our mother, lived under the same roof. It was during this period that I learnt to cook. The first palaver sauce I ever made was potato leaves. I recall that after eating it, my dad asked if it was three-days' old, suggesting that it tasted stale. Obviously, I was not the good cook I thought I was.

This was a period of transition for me in many other ways as my father's move to Freetown coincided with my admission to St. Joseph's Secondary School for Girls. At the time, it was headed by Miss Florence Dillsworth, the best school principal I have ever known. Since I loved studying, I continued to do exceptionally well at school, but once I became a teenager, I engaged in various acts of self-discovery which earned me the reputation of being troublesome. When I was fifteen, and getting ready to take my GCE 'O' level exams, I developed a passion for a charming boy, called Marc Muhlemann; he had been one of my neighbours at the PWD compound. Aunty (our mother), was still living in Bo, and while 'the king' and my sisters were not around Marc and I indulged in the kind of naughtiness that results in a girl becoming pregnant.

It was still taboo for adults to talk to adolescents about sex or the sexual organs of the human body so I had had no sex education to introduce me to this part of growing up; but I knew, from my biology textbook, that my periods stopping probably meant that I was pregnant. However, for a while, I did not apply that knowledge to what was happening to me. When I finally faced the fact that I was pregnant, I dared not tell anybody; not even my sisters, let alone 'the king', but Sentho and Yemah soon noticed the changes in my body. Being teenagers themselves they, too, did not know what to do and in the end, decided to tell Aunty Lucy to whom, unlike our mother, one could confide anything. They sent her a message to say she was needed in Freetown because something terribly important had happened. It was Aunty Lucy who broke the news to my father.

I shall never forget how shattered he was when he heard that I had got myself pregnant; it must have been like a knife wound to his chest. The king of the Woobays, whom we also jokingly called, 'Toughest', was so hurt, so deeply hurt that he was weeping as he confronted me. That was the first time I had ever seen my father cry, and those tears running down his cheeks broke my heart. Everyone in the family—my mum, my sisters, my other aunts, my uncles, and my cousins—expressed huge disappointment that I had dashed their hopes and expectations that I would pass my 'O' levels with flying colours. I spent my days in floods of tears at the thought that I had not only brought disgrace to my family but that through my foolish actions, had also ended my schooling. What sharpened my pain was that my partner in crime, hardly more than a child himself, was nowhere to be found.

Chapter Three

Tears and more tears

In our culture, children take no part in what are considered adult matters, so once I had disclosed the name of the boy who made me pregnant, my parents handled the situation. It was only some time afterwards that I learnt how things unfolded. My mum told Uncle Solo's wife, late Aunty Deborah, that a boy called Marc Muhlemann was the father of the child I was expecting. Uncle Solo, who was a practising lawyer at the time, had as a partner, the late Gervas Betts; so once she had recovered from her shock and horror, Aunty Deborah told Mrs. Betts, who happened to be related to Mrs. Muhlemann. Mrs. Betts in turn told Mrs Muhlemann, who, instead of telling her husband, made arrangements for Marc to go abroad immediately, hence his disappearance. What added to our pain was that the Muhlemanns made no attempt to contact us. In spite of the immense support my dear sisters, Sentho and Yemah gave me, I really cried. However, there is only so much crying one can do so, confused and distressed as I felt, I eventually dried my tears, and started wondering what kind of a future awaited me. Two things brought me a bit of comfort: Aunty Lucy told me that Miss Dillsworth had assured her that if I continued to study hard I could still take my 'O' level exams as planned, and Florella Hazeley, a family friend, kept telling me that all was not lost; that my parents would forgive me.

Indeed, my parents dried their own tears and started making arrangements for the help I was going to need in the months ahead. The first thing they did was to send me away from Freetown to one of my maternal aunts, Dr. Theresa Ganda, an obstetrician /gynaecologist who ran a private hospital in Kenema. Aunty Theresa took me into her home and looked after me throughout my pregnancy. She was, quite simply, my saviour; and what comforted me even more was that while I lived with her, she made sure that her entire community in Dauda Town (named after her husband Mr. J.B.Dauda), treated me as they would their own child. I shall never forget Aunty Theresa's kindness to me, nor shall I ever stop blessing her. Though we are related, I have no doubt that she would have given the same help to anybody else, such was the warmth and generosity she showed towards all the people she dealt with. It was no surprise that she had such kind-hearted and thoughtful children. Her son, Borbor Dauda, barely seven years old at the time, adopted my baby when it came; brought me all the tiny clothes his mother had kept and came to check on us every day. Sadly,

Aunty Theresa passed away while I was working on this book. May perpetual light shine on her beautiful soul.

I still vividly remember that Saturday morning at Ganda Hospital. Aunty Theresa had already decided that my pelvis was much too narrow for a normal delivery, and that she would have to do a Caesarean section before I went into labour. On hearing this my mum's face had fallen with dismay, and once again I felt terrible that I was causing her distress. Fortunately, Aunty Theresa calmed her fears, and the surgery went smoothly. At noon, on April 4th, 1987, my baby boy came into the world. We called him David Woobay, after my dad.

Two weeks after David's birth, my mother and I moved to Bo to stay with Auntie Lucy. The nights were horrible. Still in pain from the operation, I had to take care of both myself and my son; and that was hard, especially having to rouse my exhausted body at night to breastfeed. Sometimes I was so exhausted that I did not hear David's cries of hunger and my mother would wake me up with an angry shake or even a slap. She was really hard on me (bless her heart!); but I understood that no mother wants to see a daughter, who is scarcely out of childhood herself, having to care for a baby. I must confess that those early days of motherhood were almost too much for me. No matter how rough the night had been, I had wake up at daybreak to launder cloth nappies, and once the rainy season began, iron those that were still damp. And then, I had to take care of David. I lost weight, lost strength, and wept buckets of tears.

Chapter Four

Rescued

That horrible experience convinced me that no teenage girl should have to become a mother. But for the love and support my family gave me, I doubt that I would have survived the ordeal. My cousins, Mam and Mahen Fallah helped in any way they could. Coming from a distance, Mam would pop in to check on me, and Mahen, who was younger than me and did not understand much, watched me with love and helped baby-sit my son whenever she could. Once my dad, the tough king of the Woobays, regained his equilibrium, he showed me the love, kindness and mercy of a father who lived for his children. He travelled to Bo bringing disposable nappies for my son; diapers of the 'Pampers' variety, which in 1980s Sierra Leone must have cost him a small fortune. Having them lightened my chores when heavy and long lasting rain made cloth nappies difficult to dry. After David's birth, Sentho and Yemah, who had been towers of strength during my pregnancy, continued to support me by traveling from Freetown to Kenema as often as they could. Once they even brought me ice cream so that I could have another taste of city life.

Several months later, when I was living in Bo, they came to visit from Freetown again and, seeing how depressed I was, Yemah suggested that they take David away at the end of August so I could go back to school. Everyone thought it was a good idea, especially Aunty Lucy who had never stopped reminding me how important it was for me to get my 'O' levels. Needless to say, my spirits rose at once at the thought that not only would I have an opportunity to continue my education but also to regain the confidence and trust my family once had in me.

According to plan, Yemah, took five-month-old David to Freetown that September and I began to attend the Ahmadiyya Muslim School in Bo. Since I had let so many people down, a fire burned in me to succeed. Knowing what it would take for my mother to forgive me completely, I was determined to make her proud of me again. And I had to make 'the king' as proud of me as before. For a whole year all I did was study with the result that I passed my GCE 'O' levels with flying colours. My sisters were delighted for me, and my parents, jubilant. My entire family celebrated that success as Peagie's first step towards getting back on track.

Peagie 1ˢᵗ from right, front row at AWMS with
6ᵗʰ form colleagues 1989

One member of the family who had been particularly angry with me was my great uncle, Solomon Berewa. Before my disgrace, he fondly called me 'Gutu', meaning in Mende, 'shortie'. I lost that pet name for a whole year. In fact, Uncle Solo did not speak to me at all during that time, not even when I greeted him. I understood his anger and disappointment as he had played an important role in my previous excellent

23

performance at school. Whenever we spent the holidays at his home in King Tom, he never allowed having fun to take over the academic aspect of our lives, and also made sure that we had all our textbooks for the class to which we had been promoted. I did not immediately get back my pet name when I passed my GCE 'O' Levels so well, but when Uncle Solo drove me himself to enrol at the Annie Walsh Memorial School to study for my 'A' levels, I considered myself forgiven.

Some of the girls in my class at the AWMS had been my juniors at St. Joseph's and had not set eyes on me since my abrupt departure. They were glad to see me back at school and though I did not hide the fact that I was a teenage mum, they never said anything to me about it. I suppose they thought doing so might be hurtful. I remember that one girl, the late Avril Adegboyega (Avril Blyden at the time), used to ask how my son was doing and even brought me clothes

24

for him once. The teachers, too, were kind and never mentioned my status as a teenage mother.

I had a lot of help with taking care of David while I studied for my 'A' level exams and as early as possible he was enrolled in a creche and later in pre-school. Everyone in the family spoiled him, especially my dad. It was as if he had transferred the love he once had for me to his grandson. For David's first birthday my parents and sisters went all out to give him a wonderful birthday party, but I insisted on buying his birthday outfit out of money I had saved. It meant a lot for me to do that. I could not get him anything fancy, but the satisfaction of using my own money to buy him a gift brought happiness to my heart. My sole aim in life was to attain higher heights so as to give myself and my son a good life.

Chapter Five

Moving Up

After my 'A' levels, I was admitted to Fourah Bay College and moved up to Mount Aureol with the help of a grant from the Catholic mission in Sierra Leone. I started off studying English, French and Linguistics, but being always highly motivated, I did so well in French that after my third (Qualifying) year results came out, I was invited to work towards an honors degree. Before that, something wonderful happened. When David was three years old, using Mrs. Rebecca Betts as a go-between, his father's parents finally asked to meet mine and, though they had been extremely hurt by the Muhlemanns' previous behavior, my parents decided to let bygones

26

be bygones. My dad received the Muhlemann delegation at his office at the National Stadium, then arranged for them to come to the house to meet my mother. All this I learned after the events because though I was now an adult, in accordance with our culture, I was still not consulted beforehand. It was David's maternal and paternal grandparents who decided that his surname should be changed from Woobay to Muhlemann and that his father, Marc, would become financially responsible for him. David began spending time with his paternal grandparents twice a month and eventually we all became such good friends that I began to call them Uncle Marc and Aunty Melissa. Two years later, the most memorable event in my university years occurred. Marc himself paid a visit to Sierra Leone and looked me up. He claimed that he only learnt of David's existence when his parents accepted him as their first grandchild.

My undergraduate years were, on the whole, happy ones though daily life at Fourah Bay College was hard. Water shortages meant having to go to the stream to fetch what we needed for bathing and for cleaning the toilets which we often had to do ourselves since the hired cleaners could not work without water. Due to frequent power cuts, we also had to provide our own lighting and had the additional chore of preparing meals after lectures; the food provided by the college canteen, though cheap, was often inedible. My grant included a small amount for living expenses, but in those circumstances, it was hardly adequate. However, we were blessed with excellent lecturers and the existence of the French Embassy's Pedagogical Centre down in the city. This gave us access to literature we needed for our studies, unlike the university library with its mostly empty shelves and where some of our fellow students had the selfish habit of tearing the most essential pages out of books.

My roommate, Sally Williams, was a girl from the east end of Freetown, an area known as Fourah Bay. That was where the original Fourah Bay College was located, and the old building still stands. We met each other for the first time only in the room we had been given, but she was such a warm and open person that we instantly became as close as sisters. On the very day we moved in I told her my story, and it was she who suggested that I bring David up to Mount Aureol to spend some weekends with me. I took her advice and in that way was able to be both a student and a mother. I loved using some of my meagre allowance to by David ice cream.

I studied hard, but also played hard, going to all the parties at the Students Union building, taking part in debates and dramatic performances. I even played tennis on the university courts. In addition, I was an active member of social groups, like the Dahlia Club and the Azalea Sorority, and particularly enjoyed the fund-raising activities geared towards giving back to the college community. In my Qualifying year I was elected President of the Dahlia Club and as part of our programme, we provided dustbins and concrete seats for the small garden near the female hostel called Beethoven Hall. I was also a member of the Catholic Students Union.

As I mentioned earlier, I was invited to read for an honors degree in French. My class was the last batch of students to spend a year mastering the language at the expense of the French government. Cheik Anta Diop University in Dakar, Senegal, was great, with impressive library facilities, twenty-four-hour electricity and running water in the student hostels, as well as transportation into the city centre, even at night. Our grant from the French government allowed us not only to live well but also to travel within and outside Senegal; so we made time to visit the famous tourist sites on Goree and Ngor Islands, and Le Lac Rose. Being an adventurous person, I also went alone by train to Bamako, in Mali, Nouakchott in Mauritania, and by bus to Banjul in The Gambia. As part of the one-year course, I had to write a paper and chose as its subject the community in a village called Kaolak. I spent two interesting weeks there, experiencing the life and culture of the people. My paper, which I defended successfully, was entitled, 'Living simply in an increasingly modern Senegal'.

After that formative, productive and enjoyable year at Cheik Anta Diop University, I returned to Fourah Bay College, wrote my dissertation and graduated with honors. I now felt well equipped to raise my son and conquer the world.

Chapter Six

Greener Pastures

Freetown is twinned with Hull City in the UK; as a result of that, Our Lady Star of the Sea, the Catholic church in the area called Juba, is twinned with Holy Cross Catholic church in Cottingham, a small town on the outskirts of Hull. While I was a student, four visitors from that church the late Rev. Father Storey, the parish priest, and three parishioners, honoured us with a visit. A volunteer was needed to take them round and spend time with the two young girls with them. I gladly offered my services, proud to show them the beauty of my country. Ever since then, I had nursed an ambition to become a tour coordinator, but a vicious civil conflict had been raging in the hinterland and, by the time I graduated had intensified, with the demise of most, if not all, enterprises in the country. My dream of working in the tourist industry therefore had to be shelved and I decided to become a teacher instead. In 1996 I was hired at the Services Military School at Juba, but when I was told that my salary would be 130,000 Leones (worth about US$50 at the time), I realized I could not stay. How could I possibly survive on 130,000 Leones a month with transportation costs, bills to be paid, supplies to be purchased for my son, and all the demands that came with life in a country at war? That was when the shocking reality of poverty in Sierra Leone first hit me. Next, I spent two months selling advertising space to local companies for a newspaper called, 'For Di Pipul', but even then could not make an adequate living. I began to turn my thoughts towards greener pastures abroad.

As luck would have it, I heard of a French essay writing competition which was right up my street, because I loved writing essays and several years back, had won a holiday to France in another competition. This time the subject was the group of 19th Century artists whose style of painting was termed Impressionist. My essay was one of the five winning ones and as a prize we spent five weeks of the summer of 1996 visiting an Impressionist village. I had kept in touch with the Catholic parish in Cottingham and was invited to visit them during my trip to Europe. However, obtaining a Visitors Visa for the UK was a problem. When I mentioned my poor employment prospects at home, Father Storey suggested that I explore the possibility of doing further studies in Paris and offered to pay for my fees and accommodation, but not my travel expenses. I succeeded in getting a place in a college to study public administration, but had to return home for a Student Visa, which I did that September. What a blow it was when my parents told me they could not afford to pay for my ticket and visa. It took a bit of hustling and help from a generous friend in the US, but I was able to set off for Paris on 13th October, 1996. It was hard to leave David behind, but the knowledge that I was going to fight for us both strengthened my determination not to cry.

My college was in the heart of Paris. As usual, I studied hard but did not deny myself an active social life. I also did babysitting jobs so I could send some money home to help with David's upkeep. It was during my summer holiday that I met a successful French lawyer from a well-to-do family, called Phillipe Thevenard; he was divorced with two small children. Phillipe was much older than me, but we clicked at once because we both enjoyed dancing, movies, playing tennis, and travel. We eventually married, but being his wife was more of a challenge than I had anticipated. Apart from our cultural differences, his children had been badly affected by his divorce which had been a bitter one. They spent two weeks out of every month with us and it took all my people skills to win them over; but I succeeded.

In 1998 I asked Marc if David could come over to France to live with me. We did all we could to get him a visa, but without success. Finally, we obtained a single-entry, six-month Visitors Visa for him to visit his father in the UK. With that he was able to come across the channel and spend Christmas with us in Paris. We also had no problem with his re-entering UK as he had a return ticket to Freetown which we assured the immigration officials he would be using. However, we were forced to go back on our word as people advised us not to send David back home. The war in Sierra Leone was spreading and they foresaw further trouble in Freetown.

Indeed, in May, 1997 a brutal military coup had taken place and had brought rebel fighters to the capital with resulting mayhem and loss of life. So David overstayed his visa and remained in London with his dad and step-mum. He could not leave the country till his immigration status was sorted out, but with London much closer to Paris than Freetown, I was often able to hop over to visit him.

With the help of my guardian, Father Storey, we were able to get him into a Catholic school in South London. It took him a while to settle down, but he eventually did. Two years later, I was finally able to bring him over to Paris to live with us. I put him in an international school, where he learned to speak French in nine months, then moved him to a public school. It was tough for him at the beginning; having to learn a new language and adjust to a new environment yet again but thrived. And so did I, happy that I could at last give him the life he deserved. He got on well with Phillipe and his children, the younger of the two being just a couple of months his junior and for a while we were a family; but as always with life, things happen, things change. Phillipe and I eventually grew apart and divorced in 2006. The separation was amicable, though. David still considers Phillipe his step-father and remains close to his step-siblings.

I spent twelve years in Paris, working with a communications company, first as a Supervisor at their call centre, later as a Project Manager, and did a lot of travelling. Then things changed again, and my life took a completely different direction.

David at dad (Marc), Paris

Peagie and Rev Fr Storey, Hull UK

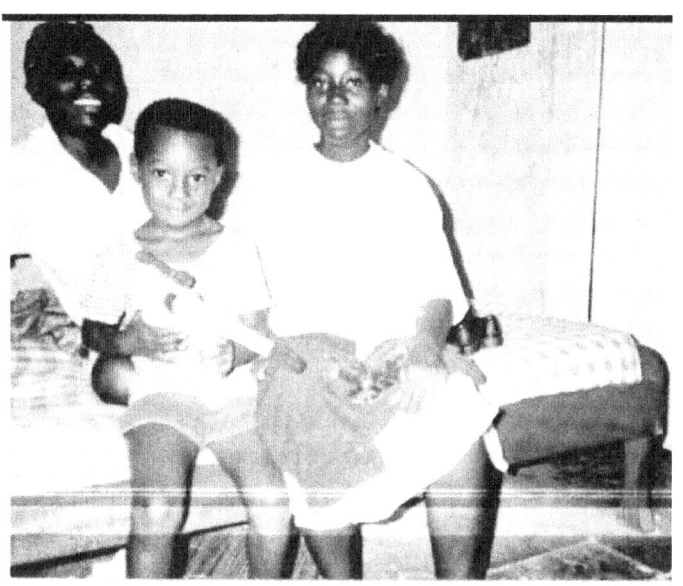

*Sentho, David & Peagie.eagie's 1ˢᵗ gift to
David on his 5ᵗʰ birthday*

David and Peagie (Paris)

Chapter Seven

Enter Mr Foday

In a way it was, 'Re-enter Mr. Foday' because I first met my second husband in primary school in Bo. Even then, Emmanuel Foday was quiet, on the stocky side, and always neatly dressed. I admired him so much that in our fifth year in primary school I sent him a love letter through a mutual friend, now deceased. Michael, as he was called, promised to give me Emmanuel's reply on condition that I shared my lunch with him, but in order to keep enjoying my bread, butter and jam sandwiches, he kept me in suspense for months. In fact, not until I was about to enter secondary school did I receive a cheeky reply that *he*, Emmanuel Foday, did not love me. That didn't matter because I moved to Freetown while he remained in Bo. Not till years later did we meet again. I had gone to visit my aunt Lucy in Bo and bumped into him. I remember that to pay him back for rejecting my previous advances, I refused his request for a kiss; we parted again and life went on. He became a footballer after his 'A' levels, and played for both Blackpool (a local team) and our national squad, the Leone Stars. He turned professional by moving to Sweden and playing for a team called Spanga IK. The next time we met, I was at university. He took me to dinner at the Chinese restaurant on Wilkinson Road and we got on well, but I refused to take our relationship any further and once again we went our separate ways though we kept in touch. He got engaged, and I got married, but then both our relationships failed and once again, we were both available. However, I had decided that marriage wasn't my cup of tea and that since David had found his feet and was doing fine, I would just live my life as a single woman.

Peagie and 'Mr Foday'

I had reckoned without Emmanuel Foday's determination. He started visiting me in Paris, and invited me to visit in Stockholm, which I did. We enjoyed each other's company hugely, sharing our childhood dreams and chuckling over reminiscences of home. Gradually my fondness for him deepened into love but still, I resisted getting married. For one thing, I was afraid of going through another pregnancy and delivery by C-section and for another, after my experience with David, I dreaded the thought of having to look after a baby without family support. Love conquered my fears to the extent that I became pregnant again. Unfortunately, I lost that pregnancy, then another, due, no doubt, to my ongoing stress. When a third pregnancy seemed to settle, I agreed to get married, which we did in October, 2007. However, I lost that pregnancy too. Our daughter, Manelle, wasn't born till September 2008.

When I became pregnant with Manelle, consulting the doctor for the first time so frightened me that I could barely let him examine me. I was afraid that he would confirm my suspicion that I could not carry another pregnancy to term. Dr. Ganda had told that my pelvis stopped growing after David's birth. My years of research on the subject and those previous miscarriages had suggested that that might indeed be my fate. The doctor calmed my fears after hearing my history and though Manelle came later than expected, all went well. However, her delivery was by a C-section, and delivery by C-section it will always be for Peagie.

We had to make a decision after Manelle's birth. I loved my job, but since Emmanuel did not speak French, I knew he would feel more comfortable as head of our family if we lived in Sweden where he could work, instead of staying home to look after our child. I also knew I would have no problem learning

Swedish and, in any case, from what I had learned on my numerous visits there, all Swedes speak English. Besides, Sweden was better than France for families. So we moved there in December, 2008 when Manella was three months old.

When love reigns, things go smoothly. I missed my beautiful Paris and the few good friends I had had to leave behind but settling down was not too difficult. I found the Swedish winter brutal but with white snow on the ground, and dark skies above, Stockholm was lovely; and since everyone spoke English, adventurous Peagie enjoyed going out by herself when Emmanuel was at work. Becoming a full-time wife and mother was another big change for me. However, I gave it my all, knowing that it was only a temporary situation.

In accordance with Swedish family law, I had to stay home for a year to look after Manelle, with a basic maternity allowance. As soon as she was one year old, I put her in a daycare centre in the neighbourhood, did one six-month course in basic Swedish for immigrants, and another in Swedish as a second language. After a year, I could babble some Swedish, so started applying for work; but I had not mastered the language sufficiently to get the kind of job I wanted, so I returned to school. When I reached a level high enough to enter university, I started looking for work again, in embassies this time, and in January 2012, I was employed as Administration and Finance Officer at the small Embassy of Malaysia. It is a small establishment but I enjoy both job satisfaction and a pleasant working environment.

With my caring husband, being a wife and mother has brought me fulfillment and given me the peace of mind to put into action a dream I had had ever since going through the experience of becoming a teenage mother: it was to help teenage girls who drop out of school due to pregnancy and do not have the support and opportunities to complete their education that I received from a strong, loving family. March is the month celebrating women. When it came round in 2013 I discussed my dream with my husband. Ever supportive, Mr. Foday gave me the thumbs up, and that was how **The Peagie Woobay Scholarship Fund**, began, with its mantra…**For love of the girls**. It has become my passion and to further its goals I give it maximum publicity during my annual vacations in Sierra Leone through Talk Shows, visits to school and various communities. Mr. Foday either accompanies me, or stays in Sweden to take care of the kids. In 2015 God blessed us with our second and last child, Emmanuel Nyakeh Elongima Foday, who is so active that we have been forced to become much more youthful than our biological ages, which is a good thing. To widen their horizons, we take him and his equally active sister, Manelle, on family excursions and trips overseas as often as we can.

Chapter Eight

The Peagie Woobay Scholarship Fund

The aim of the Peagie Woobay Scholarship Fund is to empower girls in Sierra Leone, especially teenagers. My focus is on educating them on the hazards of early pregnancy and, using my own experience, discouraging them from becoming pregnant whilst still at school. I also introduce them to strategies they could use if they do fall pregnant. The scholarship offers free secondary school tuition and includes providing uniforms and textbooks. Since I love reading and writing, I have made being able to write good English the core requirement for winning a scholarship. Contestants are judged through writing competitions whose topics I select myself. The first one was, **What every girl deserves in Sierra Leone.** The girls produced essays which I thoroughly enjoyed reading, and those who won scholarships were delighted to be rewarded for their good work.

We awarded the first five scholarships to underprivileged teenage girls in Bo, in the Southern Province and by September, 2013, had increased the number of beneficiaries to sixty-five. The other girls were chosen from most of the major towns. Among them were twenty teenage mothers for whom we opened daycare centres and employed six women to look after their kids while they were in school.

We now run regular workshops for the girls on subjects, ranging from teenage pregnancy to girl child education and early marriage. In 2014 we scaled the number of awards up to one hundred and held our first 'girls out' retreat at our centre in Kabala, in the Northern Province. Girls on our scheme, from all over the country, met for the first time. They enjoyed being away from home and the activities which included sports, poetry reading, dancing and listening to motivational speakers.

Peagie with David at his 30th birthday

Every year since 2013, we have been able to increase the number of girls we fund. The number now stands at one hundred and twenty-six. One of our first beneficiaries is now at university, reading social sciences. For love of the girls, we have diversified the project by including more activities. We now give carers at the daycare centres proper training, have structured the organization for better functioning and established a reading room and health room at our recently opened resource centre in Moyamba. These facilities provide our girls with a place to work after school and access to basic and preventive health care.

In 2015, we established a branch in the USA which, with the branches in Sweden and Sierra Leone helps raise funds to sustain our project for which I still provide 20% of the revenue. The fund-raising efforts of the branches have made a huge difference. For example, after sharing office space for three years, we now have our own office at 9 Willoughby Lane in Brookfields, Freetown and, as mentioned earler, just recently completed a resource centre for the girls in Moyamba.

David with a PWSF girl

Finding the right human resources for any project is a big challenge in Sierra Leone. People are often either lazy or reluctant to act on their own initiative. It took us two years to recruit a reliable project manager, and we have had to do a lot of on-the-job training with him; but he has has been willing to learn and is doing well. Other constraints include lack of electricity at the centres which makes providing food expensive as purchases have to be made every day. Providing sufficient lighting for the girls to study by has been another challenge. Last year we were able to provide a few solar lamps for them but not enough. One regrettable aspect of our work has been girls dropping out of the scheme as happened after the Ebola outbreak. We lost some of the girls, though not to the disease. They just did not return to the towns where they had lived before and we have been unable to trace them. Despite these challenges and setbacks, we soldier on…**for love of the girls**. Now that we know that our blueprint works, we have become even more determined to make a difference in their lives and have started writing proposals for international funding agencies. Meanwhile, I thank the Almighty for inspiring me to embark on this worthwhile project and for blessing me with the necessary strength and energy and a husband who is the wind beneath my wings.

David doing tough mudder race to raise funds for the girls. He raised £3000

Printed in Great Britain
by Amazon